Something to Talk About

Something to Talk About

A Reproducible Conversation Resource for Teachers and Tutors

Kathleen Olson

Ann Arbor
THE UNIVERSITY OF MICHIGAN PRESS

Illustrated by Nancy Brown

Acknowledgments

When I announced I was going to write a book, my contractor told me there were only two types of people in this world—those who have written a book and those who are going to. I am glad to be among the former, but I would not have gotten there without the help of many others. First I am most thankful for the encouragement and support of my children, Steve, Julie, and Kristi. Kristi, in particular, kept asking me when I was going to write my book, until I finally wrote it just to stop her from asking. I am also deeply appreciative of the suggestions and inspiration of my colleagues, particularly Jeanette Bolivar and Thelma Wurzelbacher.

Contents

Introduction 1

Part A. Personal 3
I Don't Have Anything to Wear
I'm Having a Bad Hair Day
Money Can't Buy Happiness
Don't Judge a Book by Its Cover

Part B. Family Issues 11
It's All in the Family
Are You the Baby in Your Family?
If I Told You Once, I Told You a Million Times
Don't Talk with Your Mouth Full

Part C. Home Issues 17
Home Is Where the Heart Is
Paper or Plastic?
Home Sweet Home

Part D. Health Issues 23
No Pain, No Gain
Take Two Aspirins and Call Me in the Morning
Act Your Age
Have a Heart

Part E. Education Issues 33
Teacher's Pet
Oh No! A Pop Quiz
Variety Is the Spice of Life
If You Can Read This, Thank a Teacher

Part F. Games 43
Birds of a Feather Flock Together
Which One Doesn't Belong?
Beauty Is in the Eye of the Beholder
They Have a Lot in Common

Part G. Employment Issues 53
Did You Check the Want Ads?
It's All in a Day's Work
Money Doesn't Grow on Trees
Look on the Bright Side of Things

Part H. Leisure Issues   61

The Best Things in Life Are Free
Don't Be a Couch Potato
You Get What You Pay For
There's No Such Thing as a Free Lunch

Part I. Societal Issues   67

Better Safe Than Sorry
Don't Believe Everything You Hear
You Be the Judge
One Person's Trash Is Another Person's Treasure

Part J. Cultural Issues   73

All Good Things Must Come to an End
Silence Is Golden
Finders Keepers, Losers Weepers
Do You Swear to Tell the Truth?

Part K. Choices   81

Once Upon a Time
You Can't Have Your Cake and Eat It Too
A Penny for Your Thoughts
And They All Lived Happily Ever After

Part L. Travel Issues   89

Everything but the Kitchen Sink
It's a Small, Small World
It's a Lemon
Mirror, Mirror on the Wall, Who's the Fairest
    of Them All?
Tell It Like It Is

Part M. Life Changes   97

For Better or for Worse
Baby Talk
Here Today, Gone Tomorrow
Gone but Not Forgotten

Introduction

Something to Talk About is a 13-part conversation resource book for adults and young children at the intermediate and advanced levels. This book provides students with discussion generators on many interesting and engaging topics that can be used to practice speaking and listening skills and to develop fluency in English. Each part focuses on a universally common theme, asking students to talk about their own knowledge and experiences, thereby reducing their need to master new content while developing communicative competence. The conversations are based on students' lives and interests since research indicates that students learn faster and retain more when the content is meaningful and pertinent to them.

Included within each activity are interesting facts about American culture. Students learning a new language and living in a new culture immediately notice differences and similarities between the new culture and their native cultures. Activities in *Something to Talk About* give students a chance to share their observations and to learn more about American culture while simultaneously providing an interesting and informative learning experience for the listener. Many activities are titled with a common American saying or proverb, so that students have the opportunity to learn American aphorisms and to share similar adages from their cultures.

Something to Talk About activities can be used in a variety of situations. The material is appropriate for use as a primary text in a conversation class, as a supplemental text in a combined-skills adult education class, as a source of warm-up activities in an intensive English class, or as a conversational framework for tutor-student or Conversation Partner programs. As the purpose of this book is to generate discussions and conversations in which the students do a lot of talking, the use of many open-ended questions and the pertinent content of the activities are designed to keep conversation flowing. In addition, the activities in *Something to Talk About* are not sequential. Teachers, tutors, or conversation partners can decide in which order to use them based on student interests, usefulness to students, or relevance to other class instruction.

Something to Talk About is unique in that the activities in the book require no teacher preparation or instruction. The activities are designed to be done in pairs or small groups to ensure that each student will have the greatest opportunity to speak and to more closely replicate natural conversational situations. The activities can be done with non-native speakers, native-speaker pairs, or two or more non-native speakers together. There is sufficient material within each activity to accommodate the quicker learners. As the goal of this book is to generate student-centered conversations leading to improved communication skills, it is not necessary to complete an activity, only to converse. So, give your students *Something to Talk About!*

Part A
PERSONAL

I Don't Have Anything to Wear

Talk about a favorite piece of clothing.

- What does it look like?
- When did you get it?
- Why do you like it?

Have you ever worn a costume?

Describe the most unusual thing you have ever worn.

What are some differences in clothing between the United States and your country?

- In fabrics?
- In sizes?
- In colors?
- In styles?

Do men and women wear the same styles in your country?

What styles are popular with teenagers in your country?

What kinds of jewelry do people in your country wear?

Describe what you would wear to

- a wedding
- a funeral
- a special event
- school
- work

I'm Having a Bad Hair Day

What are your feelings about your hair? Are you satisfied with it?

_____

Only 7% of Americans say they wouldn't change a thing about their hair. The rest say it is either too curly or too straight, too thick or too thin, too oily or too dry, or the wrong color.

_____

Have you had problems with your hair?

How do you treat it? Do you do anything special to your hair?

The average American woman spends 16.5 minutes styling her hair each day. Men spend 7.6 minutes.

_____

Discuss any rules your school had about hairstyles.

Who makes the decisions concerning your hair?

What is the biggest event in the life of your hair?

Do most people in your country have the same color hair?

_____

Only 2% of Americans are redheads; the rest have blonde, brunette, brown, or black hair.

_____

Do people in your country color their hair?

What percent of people in the United States do you think color their hair?*

_____

* In the United States, 34% of women and 6% of men color their hair.

Money Can't Buy Happiness

What is happiness?

Tell about ten things that make you happy.

What things made you happy as a child?

What do you think will give you pleasure in your future?

What age-group do you think is the happiest?*

Would these things make you happy? Why or why not?

    The smell of coffee

        New babies

        Getting tickets to a play

    Feeding ducks on the river

        Goodnights

    Flying kites

        Long-distance calls

  Sunday naps

        Starry nights

        Cuddly white rabbits

    Taking care of plants

        Graduations

        Watching the sun rise

What things can you do to make other people happy?

---

*In the United States, 39% of those over 65 say they are very happy, compared to only 28% of those 18–39 years of age.

Don't Judge a Book by Its Cover

What are the best reasons to marry someone?

Who chooses your spouse?

How do you get to know each other?

Does your culture value certain qualities above others in a mate?

With a partner, list the qualities that are most important to each of you in selecting a mate. Circle the one that is most important to you.

You	Your Partner

What quality did you list as most important?

_____

According to one poll reported in _USA Today,_ women said the most
important quality in a potential spouse or significant other is

emotional warmth and nurturing	50% of women
a sense of humor	25% of women
intelligence	15% of women
confidence/power	5% of women
physical appearance	3% of women
money/wealth	2% of women

(Information from Maritz Poll, February 1999: "The American Love-o-Meter: Less than Half
Say It's Red Hot," _USA Today._)

_____

Do you think women look for different qualities in a mate than do men?

In what order do you think men in the _USA Today_ poll listed the qualities?

_____

Forty-three percent of men thought emotional warmth was the most
important quality, while 22% favored intelligence and 6% favored physical
appearance.

(Information from as above.)

_____

Part B
FAMILY ISSUES

It's All in the Family

Describe the members of your household.

Which of the following family types best describes your family?

- A nuclear family—a father and mother and their children
- An extended family—the nuclear family plus other family members, such as grandparents
- A blended family—one or two remarried partners and their children from any previous marriages
- A single-parent household—one parent and his or her children.

Which is the most common family type in your country?

_____

In the United States, 27% of families with children are single-parent families; 2 million of them are headed by a single father.

_____

What are some advantages and disadvantages of the different family types?

Share some memories of your grandparents or other relatives.

What is the past history of your family?

What is the history of your family name?

Are You the Baby in Your Family?

Who are the people in your family?

What position do you have in your family—oldest, middle, youngest, or only child?

What are the advantages and disadvantages of being in your position in the family?

Describe your personality.

Do you think your birth position has affected your personality? If so, in what ways?

Research in the United States shows that
- the oldest child is *usually*

conscientious and reliable	a leader
a perfectionist	an achiever

- the middle child is *usually*

the one with the most friends	a peacemaker
more relaxed	even-tempered

- the youngest child is *usually*

charming and playful	creative
happy to be the center of attention	

- the only child is *usually*

self-confident	often a leader
a good student	well organized

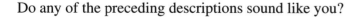

Do any of the preceding descriptions sound like you?

Do you notice any of these characteristics in your siblings or children?

What are some other factors that can affect one's personality?

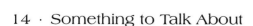

If I Told You Once, I Told You a Million Times

Discuss your thoughts on having and raising children.

- Is having a child necessary for a fulfilling life?
- What is the best way to raise a child?
- What is the most difficult aspect of raising a child?

There are three main types of parenting styles.

- *Authoritarian*—the parents make all decisions.
- *Democratic*—the children are involved in making decisions.
- *Permissive*—the children make all decisions.

What was your parents' parenting style?

Which style will you use to raise your children? Why?

Were you spoiled as a child?

Give three examples of spoiling a child.

Should children receive an allowance? Why?

What chores should children be expected to do?

What rules did children or teenagers have to follow in your childhood home?

How should children be disciplined?

- What types of punishment are okay?
- Should children be spanked?

Describe a time when you were punished.

Don't Talk with Your Mouth Full

Describe a typical meal at home in your country.

- How does it differ from a typical American meal?
- How is the food served?
- Is color important when serving the meal?
- Is there a seating arrangement at the table?
- What is discussed at the table?
- What beverages are served?

At what times are meals usually eaten in your country?

In your country, is a dessert usually eaten after dinner?

What are some common foods and drinks in your country or region?

Which of these are good for your health and which are probably bad for you?

Are there certain foods your country is known for?

What is the food you miss most from your country?

What is your favorite food and how is it prepared?

Do you use a recipe? If so, how is the recipe recorded?

Part C
HOME ISSUES

Home Is Where the Heart Is

Who lived in your childhood home?

Who did most of the chores?

> Did you have some chores to do? If so, what were they, and what happened if you didn't do them?

Who worked outside the home?

Who took care of you?

- Who put you to bed? Discuss any bedtime rituals.
- Who took you to school?
- Who disciplined you if you misbehaved?

What did you do to have fun in your family?

What are some other things a family can do to be happy together?

What makes a house a home?

- Sounds?
- Furnishings?
- People?
- Smells?

Talk about a special memory of your childhood.

Paper or Plastic?

Who shops for groceries in your family and how often?

_____

In the United States, 78% of grocery shopping is done by women.

_____

How is shopping here different from shopping in your country?

- Produce selection?   • Freshness?
- Price?   • Quantity?
- Shopping carts?   • Types of markets?

At the grocery store, do you buy only what you came for?

- Do you buy lots of things you didn't plan to buy?
- Do you buy things you don't need now because they are on sale?
- Do you use coupons?

_____

60–70% of what people buy in grocery stores consists of items they didn't come in for.

_____

Talk about your last trip to the grocery store. List what you think are the top ten items purchased in grocery stores in the United States and in your country.

United States	Your Country

When you have completed your lists, look at the next page.

The top ten items purchased in the United States are

- · Marlboro cigarettes
- · Coca-Cola Classic
- · Pepsi Cola
- · Kraft processed cheese
- · Diet Coke
- · Campbell's soup
- · Budweiser beer
- · Tide detergent
- · Folger's coffee
- · Winston cigarettes

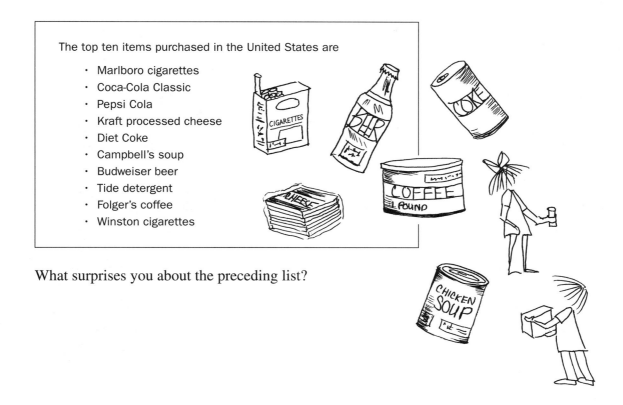

What surprises you about the preceding list?

Home Sweet Home

Describe your childhood home.

Describe the house of your dreams.

- Where is it?
- What does it look like?
- What factors are most important in selecting your dream home?

_____

The factors most important to Americans in selecting their dream homes are

- size of house
- price
- appearance
- investment value
- size of yard
- proximity to work

_____

Are the preceding factors for selecting a dream home the same as yours?

Is a garden important to you?

What interior features are most desirable to you?

_____

Inside the home, storage space, a fireplace, an entertainment center, and a pantry are considered most desirable by Americans.

_____

Part D

HEALTH ISSUES

No Pain, No Gain

How often do you exercise?

What kinds of exercises do you do?

What exercises are common in your country?

What kinds of exercising do you see Americans do that are different from those done in your country?

What percent of people do you think exercise in your country? In the United States?*

What percent of people do you think are overweight in your country? In the United States?**

Why do you think this is so?

What do you think are the benefits of regular exercise?***

Describe a simple exercise your partner can do at home.

---

*According to the U.S. Public Health Service, 35% of people in the United States exercise every day.

**Thirty-four percent of adult Americans and 25% of American children are overweight.

***According to the American Heart Association, exercise

reduces risk of heart disease	boosts energy
improves cholesterol levels	strengthens muscles
keeps weight under control	lowers blood pressure
prevents bone loss	increases self-esteem
improves sleep	reduces stress

Take Two Aspirins and Call Me in the Morning

What things do you do to stay healthy?

_____

> To help maintain health, the U.S. surgeon general recommends
> - maintaining correct weight
> - exercising regularly
> - eating a proper diet

What habits do you have that are bad for your health?

Talk about the last time you were sick.

If you do get sick, health care is private and expensive in the United States. How is health care provided and paid for in your country?

_____

> In the United States, the average person visits a doctor six times a year and spends $2,000 a year on health care.
> 83% of Americans have insurance to help pay medical bills.

_____

Describe some of the medical treatments available in your country.

In the U.S., only a limited number of medicines are available without a prescription. How do you obtain medicines in your country?

People have special remedies for treating illnesses like headaches, colds, and sore throats.

> What are some remedies your mother used for your headaches, colds, or sore throats?

Act Your Age

How long do you expect to live? Why? What factors influenced your answer?

How old was your oldest relative? Is that important?

What advice have you heard about how to live a long life?

List the factors you think influence a person's chance for a long and healthy life in your country and in the United States. Do the lists differ?

United States	Your Country

List five recommendations you would make to a person who wanted to live to be 100 years old.

1. _____
2. _____
3. _____
4. _____
5. _____

When you have completed your list, turn to the next page.

The most important factor in living a long life is to choose your parents carefully. Your heredity is very important in your longevity. Genetic factors account for about 30 percent of the differences in life expectancies. Seventy percent is up to you and what you do.

Here are several simple things people can do to increase their chances of living a long life.

1. Stop smoking—of the about 2.3 million deaths in the United States each year, 434,000 are related to smoking, making smoking the leading cause of death.
2. Eat correctly—eat more fruits and vegetables, less fat.
3. Exercise regularly—perform regular moderate physical exercise.
4. Drive carefully—about 42,000 people are killed in traffic accidents every year.
5. Maintain social contacts—people with wider social networks seem to have more resistance to disease.

Do you agree with the preceding list?

Did you think of other factors that are important for longevity?*

What do you think the life expectancy is in your country? In the United States?

See the next page for some life expectancies around the world.

---

*Did you think of these?

- Reduce stress.
- Stay active.
- Laugh a lot.
- Think positively.
- Beware of environmental factors.
- Get an annual checkup.
- Be the right gender (women live longer than men).

- Drink less alcohol.
- Maintain a healthy body weight.
- Have a sense of being in control.
- Own a pet.
- Help others.
- Get enough sleep.
- Get married (married people live longer than singles) .

Global Life Expectancies in Years		
	Men	*Women*
World Average	**61**	**64**
Latin America	64	71
United States	73	79
Australia	74	81
Asia	62	64
Africa	51	54
Europe	73	79

Have a Heart

Name as many body organs as you can.*

Do you want to donate your organs after your death? Why?

Would you agree to donate the organs of a loved one at death?

Should organ donation be required at death?

Twenty percent of Americans say they are "likely" to become an organ donor, but 78% say they would "very likely" agree to donate the organs of a loved one.

You have two kidneys and need only one. Are there any circumstances when you would donate or sell one of your kidneys?

- To save the life of a close friend or family member?
- To save the life of an elderly person?
- To save the life of a stranger?

---

* Did you think of these?

· Eyes	· Ears
· Heart	· Tongue
· Liver	· Nose
· Kidneys	· Small intestine
· Spleen	· Large intestine
· Lungs	· Bladder
· Pancreas	· Uterus
· Gall bladder	· Ovaries
· Brain	· Testes

Should people needing money be able to sell a kidney?

Does it matter what the money is for?

- To buy a Porsche?
- To go on vacation?
- To pay a family member's medical expenses?
- To pay for necessities in one's life?

Should the government have the right to prevent you from selling your organs?

The United States, Canada, and most of Western Europe have laws against the buying and selling of organs.

There are many more people needing organs than there are organs available.

- How should the person who gets an organ be determined?
- What suggestions can you give to help solve the organ shortage problem?

Which one of the following types of research do you think should be done if there is a limited amount of money?

- Research into ailments that affect a very large number of people but are not life-threatening, such as headaches, arthritis, or flu?
- Research into ailments that affect fewer people but could lead to death, such as cancer or heart disease?
- Research into ailments that affect a very small number of people but will lead to death, such as organ transplants?

Why?

Discuss your feelings about cloning.

Part E
EDUCATION ISSUES

Teacher's Pet

Describe the best teacher you ever had. What characteristics made this teacher the best for you?

Describe the worst teacher you ever had. What characteristics made this teacher the worst for you?

Do you think the characteristics of good and bad teachers are the same in the United States as in your country?

With a partner, list what you think are the five most important characteristics of good teachers.

1. _____

2. _____

3. _____

4. _____

5. _____

What do you think teachers identify as the most important characteristic of good teachers?

- Do you think it is different from what students identify?
- Do you think it is different in the United States from what it would be in your country? Why?

When you have completed this discussion, turn to the next page.

Here are the five most important characteristics of effective instructors as identified by American students in many research studies. They are not in the correct order of importance. Decide in what order you think students placed them. Put a number 1 beside the most important characteristic, a number 2 beside the next, and so on.

_____ explains content clearly
_____ stimulates student thought and interest
_____ shows enthusiasm
_____ is prepared and organized
_____ displays knowledge and love of the content

Does this list of characteristics match your list?

Do you think teachers in the studies placed the characteristics in the same order? If not, which characteristic do you think the teachers ranked first?

When you have completed your list, see the next page for the actual rankings.

The students in the studies identified "shows enthusiasm" as the most important characteristic of a good teacher, followed by

2. is prepared and organized
3. stimulates student thought and interest
4. explains content clearly
5. displays knowledge and love of the content

The teachers identified "displays knowledge and love of the content" as the most important characteristic.

Oh No! A Pop Quiz

How old were you when you first began school?

How did you get to school?

Did one of your parents go with you the first day?

Describe the clothes that you usually wore to school.

Did you bring your lunch? Go home to eat? Buy your lunch?

What were some of the classroom rules?

How did teachers reprimand disobedient children? Do you think teachers should be able to spank children?

What did you like best about your school?

Describe your typical school day.

How many days do you think students should go to school?

- How many days do they go in the United States?
- How many days do they go in your country?

What do you think are the advantages and disadvantages of longer school days and years?

This list shows some differences in length of school year around the world.

Country	Length of School Year	Country	Length of School Year
China	251 days	Switzerland	207
Japan	243	Netherlands	200
Korea	220	Scotland	200
Israel	215	Thailand	200
Germany	210	United States	180
Russia	210		

Discuss other differences in schooling in your country and in the United States.

Talk about courses offered, schedules, and graduation requirements.

Variety Is the Spice of Life

Circle the number of the answer you are most likely to do in each situation.

You are going to visit your friends at their house for the first time. Do you want them to

1. write the directions?
2. tell you the directions?
3. drive and let you follow them to their house?

At work, the boss tells you to do something new on the computer. Would you prefer to

1. read about how to do it before you start?
2. ask someone to tell you how to do it?
3. just start trying to do it?

It is time to do the weekly food shopping. Do you
1. make a list of everything you need?
2. make no list but tell yourself what you need to buy?
3. walk around in the grocery store picking up things you think you need?

You are studying for a test in school. What works best for you?

1. Reading the material many times.
2. Talking to classmates or a teacher about the material.
3. Writing down the material you want to remember.

You are planning to buy a new stereo. Other than price, what would most influence your decision?

1. Reading a good review of it.
2. Hearing a friend rave about it.
3. Operating it and listening to it in the store.

How many of your answers are number 1? _____

number 2? _____

number 3? _____

When you have recorded the quantity of each number, turn to the next page.

If the majority of your responses are

- number 1, you are a visual learner. You learn best through the eye, from seeing or reading information (from books, the chalkboard, movies, etc.).

- number 2, you are an auditory learner. You learn best through the ear, from hearing words spoken, either by you or by others.

- number 3, you are a kinesthetic learner. You learn best through touch or movement, by being involved physically, by being an active participant, by doing things.

- Visual learners make up about 60% of the U.S. population.
- Auditory learners make up around 30% of the U.S. population and tend to be female.
- Kinesthetic learners make up around 10% of the U.S. population and tend to be male.

What type of learner are you?

What kinds of activities could you do to help you learn English more quickly?

Which learning style do you think does best in school in the United States? In your country? Why?

Talk about the advantages and disadvantages of each style.

Describe people you know who might be each learning type.

If You Can Read This, Thank a Teacher

How much reading do you do?

_____

Eighty-five percent of Americans report reading at least one book a year.

_____

Discuss some of your favorite activities. Is reading one of them?

_____

Twenty-seven percent of Americans list reading as one of their favorite leisure-time activities.

(Information from Yankelovich Partners poll for Reba's First Book Club.)

_____

What types of reading do you do?

_____

Americans' top choice in reading is mysteries, followed by romance fiction as the choice of one-third of American adults. Adolescents prefer to read science fiction, fantasy, and horror.

(Information from as above.)

_____

Would you prefer to read a book or watch a movie of the same story? Why?

Where do you get your reading material?

_____

Forty-one percent of Americans buy their books at bookstores. Twenty-five percent borrow their books from the library.
Electronic books are expected to comprise 10% of book sales by 2005.

(Information from as above.)

_____

Describe the procedure for using a library in your country.

When you were a child, who read to you the most?

_____

Fifty-six percent of Americans say their mothers read to them the most.

(Information from as above.)

_____

Tell one of your favorite childhood stories.

Did you ever read or hear read any of the following seven top-selling children's books? Describe the circumstances.

- *The Tale of Peter Rabbit*
- *Green Eggs and Ham*
- *One Fish, Two Fish, Red Fish, Blue Fish*
- *The Outsiders*
- *Hop on Pop*
- *Dr. Seuss's ABC*
- *The Cat in the Hat*

Part F
GAMES

Birds of a Feather Flock Together

List as many things as you can think of that fit the categories below. For example, if the category were "things that are green," possible answers would be

trees   money   seasick passengers
grocers   eyes   grass
envy   thumbs

1. Foods that are white: _____

2. Things that come in twos: _____

3. Things you find in or on trees: _____

4. Things in a doctor's office: _____

5. Things to do with a friend: _____

6. Things in a student's backpack: _____

7. Things that are often washed: _____

8. Things that are hot: _____

9. Things that are opened: _____

10. Things that run: _____

11. Ways to travel: _____

12. Jobs that don't use computers: _____

When you have completed your list, turn to the next page.

Some possible answers to the categories follow.

1. Foods that are white: bread, pasta, milk, vanilla ice cream, turnips, marshmallows
2. Things that come in twos: socks, eyes, animals on Noah's ark, hands, couples
3. Things you find in or on trees: clothes, shoes, families, nests, ribbons, trail markers, leaves
4. Things in a doctor's office: receptionist, scales, stethoscope, examining table, magazines
5. Things to do with a friend: shop, talk to on the phone, have an ice cream sundae, E-mail
6. Things in a student's backpack: food, tissue, umbrella, last week's homework, keys, gum wrappers
7. Things that are often washed: hair, cars, lettuce, dogs, hands, clothes, faces, floors, dishes, windows
8. Things that are hot: topics, colors, the sun, dogs, potatoes, wings, spicy foods
9. Things that are opened: cans, eyes, doors, windows, a mouth, Broadway shows, books, your mind
10. Things that run: machines, stockings, dyes, racers, marathoners, computer programs
11. Ways to travel: hot-air balloon, canoe, cable car, horseback, rollerblades
12. Jobs that don't use computers: gardener, cook, housekeeper

Which One Doesn't Belong?

Look at each of the following sets of four items. Think of reasons why any item in each set might not belong. There are many possible answers. For example, if the items were *books, ball, badminton, roller skates,* some possible answers would be

Books don't belong because they are not sports related.
Roller skates doesn't belong as it is two words.
Badminton doesn't belong as it is an activity that takes more than one person.
Roller skates don't belong as they don't start with *b*.

1. Dog, cow, chicken, pig

2. Doctor, dentist, nurse, veterinarian

3. Baseball, bowling, volleyball, basketball

4. Train, plane, bus, motorcycle

5. Engineer, economist, musician, ecologist

6. Apple, banana, cherry, strawberry

7. August, September, October, November

8. Dishwasher, microwave, refrigerator, dryer

9. Shirt, socks, pants, shoes

10. Teacher, nurse, policeman, astronaut

11. Potatoes, peas, peppers, broccoli

12. Glasses, earrings, ball cap, gloves

When you have completed the exercise,
turn to the next page.

Some possible answers to which one doesn't belong follow.

1. Dog, cow, chicken, pig
   - A chicken has only two legs.
   - A dog isn't an American food product.
   - A dog isn't a farm animal.
   - A chicken isn't a mammal.

2. Doctor, dentist, nurse, veterinarian
   - A veterinarian doesn't work with humans.
   - A nurse doesn't require more than four years of education.
   - A dentist doesn't carry a stethoscope.

3. Baseball, bowling, volleyball, basketball
   - *Volleyball* doesn't begin with *b*.
   - Baseball uses a small ball.
   - Bowling is not played with the ball in the air.
   - Bowling can be played alone.

4. Train, plane, bus, motorcycle
   - A motorcycle holds only one or two people.
   - A motorcycle is not commercial.
   - A plane travels in the air.
   - A train doesn't use gasoline.

5. Engineer, economist, musician, ecologist
   - In *engineer,* the final syllable is stressed.
   - A musician is not a scientist.
   - *Musician* doesn't begin with *e*.

6. Apple, banana, cherry, strawberry
   - A strawberry doesn't grow on a tree.
   - An apple is not in a banana split.
   - A banana is not red.
   - You can't eat the skin of a banana.

7. August, September, October, November
   - August doesn't contain an American holiday.
   - August is not a fall month.
   - *August* doesn't end in *–ber*.
   - *November* doesn't contain a *t*.

8. Dishwasher, microwave, refrigerator, dryer
   - A dryer is not a kitchen appliance.
   - A refrigerator doesn't heat.
   - A refrigerator doesn't have a timer.
   - A dishwasher uses water.

9. Shirt, socks, pants, shoes
   - A shirt isn't a pair.
   - *Pants* doesn't start with *s*.
   - Shoes aren't clothing.
   - A shirt isn't worn on the bottom half of the body.

10. Teacher, nurse, policeman, astronaut
    - An astronaut is not a social-service profession.
    - A teacher doesn't wear a uniform.
    - An astronaut doesn't work on Earth.

11. Potatoes, peas, peppers, broccoli
    - Potatoes grow in the ground.
    - Potatoes are not green.
    - *Broccoli* doesn't begin with *p*.
    - The plural of *broccoli* is not formed with *s*.

12. Glasses, earrings, ball cap, gloves
    - Gloves are not worn on the head.
    - A ball cap is not a pair.
    - Earrings are not functional.
    - *Gloves* has no double letter.

Beauty Is in the Eye of the Beholder

Select a person in the room and speculate about the background of that person.

Rich or poor?	Young or old?
Educated or uneducated?	Indoor worker or outdoor worker?
Active or sedentary?	Friendly or closed?
Extrovert or introvert?	Cautious or daring?
Neat or messy?	Caring or insensitive?
Interesting or dull?	Involved or bored?

What makes you think the things you do?

What might people say if they looked at you?

How are people here and in your country alike?

How are they different?

What are some characteristics of other people that attract you?

Do those characteristics remind you of other people that you know?

They Have a Lot in Common

What do the things in each of the following groups have in common?

1. Basketball players, tales, redwood trees, skyscrapers

2. Bruises, jeans, the sky, the sea, eyes, sad people, the moon

3. Camel, pyramid, desert, Cleopatra, Nile River

4. Alarm clocks, doorbells, ears, a telephone, cash registers

5. Spaghetti, belt, train, rope, Chile, yardstick, monkey's tail

6. Traffic, lead, rain, load, overweight people, duty

7. Stockings, machines, racers, dyes, dragsters, marathoners

8. Smith, Johnson, Williams, Brown, Jones

9. Letters, papers, checks, your own ticket, wills

10. Robins, coins, plates, balls, steaks

11. Clouds, balloons, wood, cork, bobbers

12. Guns, firecrackers, alarm clocks, fire engines, car horns

13. Airplanes, kites, insects, trapeze artists, birds

14. Stamps, lollipops, cat's paws, chops, salt

15. Exercisers, rubber bands, truth, balloons

See the next page for the answers.

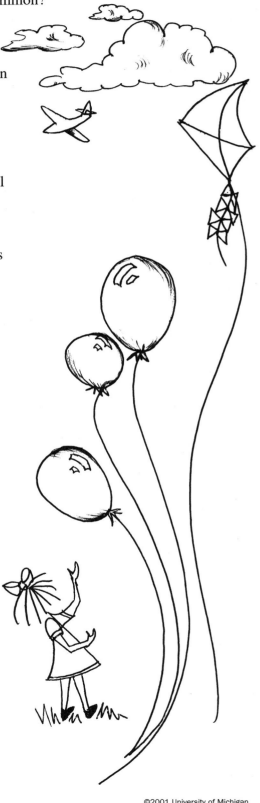

Answers to the commonalities follow.

1. Basketball players, tales, redwood trees, skyscrapers—things that are tall
2. Bruises, jeans, the sky, the sea, eyes, sad people, the moon—things that are blue
3. Camel, pyramid, desert, Cleopatra, Nile River—things found in Egypt
4. Alarm clocks, doorbells, ears, a telephone, cash registers—things that ring
5. Spaghetti, belt, train, rope, Chile, yardstick, monkey's tail—things that are long and thin
6. Traffic, lead, rain, load, overweight people, duty—things that are heavy
7. Stockings, machines, racers, dyes, dragsters, marathoners—things that run
8. Smith, Johnson, Williams, Brown, Jones—the most common surnames in the United States
9. Letters, papers, checks, your own ticket, wills—things you write
10. Robins, coins, plates, balls, steaks—things that are round
11. Clouds, balloons, wood, cork, bobbers—things that float
12. Guns, firecrackers, alarm clocks, fire engines, car horns—things that make noise
13. Airplanes, kites, insects, trapeze artists, birds—things that fly
14. Stamps, lollipops, cat's paws, chops, salt—things that are licked
15. Exercisers, rubber bands, truth, balloons—things that stretch

Part G
EMPLOYMENT ISSUES

Did You Check the Want Ads?

Describe your experiences looking for a job in your country or in the United States.

How do you think most people find jobs in your country?

- Through help-wanted newspaper advertisements?
- On the Internet?
- By networking?
- Through employment agencies?
- By cold calls (inquiring at places where you might want to work)?

In the United States, only 14% of jobs are filled through help-wanted advertising. Most U.S. jobs are filled through networking.

Most jobs require an interview. How would you answer these common interview questions? With a partner, play the role of the interviewer or interviewee.

Tell me about yourself.

Why do you want to work for us?

Why should we hire you?

What do you plan to be doing five years from now?

What are your strengths?

What are your weaknesses?

What work experience do you have?

What have you learned from your previous work experience?

What do you do if you can't find the answer to a problem?

It's All in a Day's Work

What hours do most people work in your country?

Do they change jobs or careers often?

_____

In the United States, people usually work from 8 A.M. to 5 P.M. Most
people go to a workplace, but some people work at home.
The average American changes jobs every three years and changes
careers two or three times in a lifetime.

_____

How much vacation time do workers get?

_____

The average American gets 2.8 weeks of paid vacation each year.

_____

Who decides how much the pay will be?

Are there any government regulations about pay?

_____

The U.S. government sets the minimum wage. It
was increased to $5.15 an hour in 1997.

_____

What are some common jobs for men and women in your country?

Are there jobs that are only for men or only for women?

What are some jobs you would or wouldn't like to do?

Which professions in your country are considered the most or least prestigious? Most or least honest?

> In the United States, nurses, doctors, pharmacists, clergy, and teachers are considered the most honest by the American people; lawyers, HMO managers, insurance salespeople, telemarketers, and used-car salespeople are considered the least honest.

At what age do older people usually stop working in your country?

    Do they receive retirement money from their former employer or the government?

Describe some activities people enjoy when they are retired.

Money Doesn't Grow on Trees

Describe the sizes, shapes, and colors of your country's coins and paper money.

Describe your spending habits.

What is your biggest problem with money?

Where do you carry your money when you go out? In a wallet, a purse, or your pocket?

    How is it organized?

What else do you always take with you when you go out?

Do you use checks? Debit cards? Credit cards?

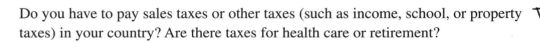

The average American adult has nine credit cards.

How do people in your country bank, make major purchases (such as a house or car), and pay bills? Do they use checks, debit cards, or credit cards?

What are the advantages and disadvantages of credit cards?

Do you have to pay sales taxes or other taxes (such as income, school, or property taxes) in your country? Are there taxes for health care or retirement?

What percent of income goes to taxes in your country?

What are some benefits you get from tax money?

Look on the Bright Side of Things

Have you ever had a job? If so, describe it.

- Did you like it?
- How did you get it?

With a partner, list the factors you think would contribute to happiness in a job.

Which factors are most important to you?
Which factors are least important to you?

Would the factors be the same in the United States and in your native country?

Most Important Factors	Least Important Factors

The ten most important factors determining job satisfaction for workers in North Carolina state government are

- fair treatment
- good benefits
- being treated with respect
- job security
- a good supervisor
- a sense of personal achievement
- a good working relationship with peers
- trust between workers and management
- pay
- the opportunity to learn

86% of the North Carolina workers said fair treatment was the most important.

How do the preceding factors from North Carolina compare with yours?

The North Carolina workers ranked the physical work environment as the least important factor.

Do you agree with that ranking? Why?

Part H
LEISURE ISSUES

The Best Things in Life Are Free

What are some of the best things in life that are free or are inexpensive?

Tell about two things you have done from this list. Then tell about two things you would like to do from this list.

go shopping
walk in a park
visit a museum
go to a class
eat in a restaurant

watch a sports activity
go biking
stop at a garage sale
share a video
fly a kite

share cooking lessons
go bowling
go to an amusement park
play a game
sit and chat

attend a cultural event
share photo albums
work in a garden
go on a picnic
visit a zoo

go to a party
go skiing
do handicrafts
visit a library
try wall climbing

Discuss other activities you would like to do in your lifetime.

Don't Be a Couch Potato

How much time do you spend watching television?

Ninety-eight percent of American homes have at least one television set, and Americans spend more than 30 hours a week watching it. Canadians average 23 hours per week in front of their television sets.

Describe some television programs you enjoy watching.

What do you like and dislike about television?

How is U.S. television different from television in your country?

What kinds of television shows are most popular on weeknights in the United States, and are these shows similar to shows in your country?

Do you like to watch game shows? Why?

Are television game shows popular in your country?
Describe some game shows in your country.

Should producers be allowed to show anything they want on television?

Are there some subjects that are not allowed in your country?

What are three advantages and three disadvantages of television for adults?
For children?

You Get What You Pay For

How is shopping in your country different from shopping in North America?

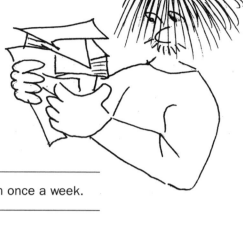

- Which items are cheaper?
- Which items are more expensive?
- Which items are not available?
- Which items are better?
- How do people pay for items?
- Are sales clerks the same?

How often do people shop in your country?

Nearly half (46%) of all Americans go shopping more than once a week.

Do people bargain or are prices marked and fixed in your country?

- Are strangers charged a different price?
- What items can you bargain for?

In the United States, it is common to bargain on cars and houses.

What is something you bought recently that was a good bargain?

What is the worst purchase you have ever made?

Does your country have sales? Coupons?

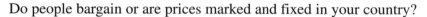

Can you return items bought in your country?

Have you ever returned anything? What? Why?

Do people in your country shop by mail? The Internet? Catalogues?

There's No Such Thing as a Free Lunch

How often do you eat in a restaurant?

_____

In the United States, 98% of families eat out at least once a month.

_____

What kind of restaurant do you usually eat at?

_____

Fifty-six percent of Americans eat at a fast-food restaurant at least once a week, 80% at least once a month.

_____

Which meal are you most likely to eat out?

_____

Forty-nine percent of Americans eat lunch out; 32% eat dinner out; 10% eat snacks out; 8% eat breakfast out.

_____

What foods do you frequently order?

_____

Foods Americans most frequently order are

- hamburgers/cheeseburgers
- french fries
- steak
- pizza
- fried chicken

Soft drinks, coffee, and iced tea are the beverages most frequently ordered.

_____

Name some of the different types of restaurants in your area.

Which one is your favorite? Talk about the last time you ate at this restaurant.

What are some differences between restaurants in your country and in the United States?

Besides food, what things make a restaurant good?

If you owned a restaurant, what kinds of food would you serve?

Part I
SOCIETAL ISSUES

Better Safe Than Sorry

Name some environmental problems in the world today.*

Describe some environmental problems in your homeland.

- Which ones are the most serious?
- What are some ways these problems can be solved?
- Are the people or the government doing anything to correct them?

Who do you think should be responsible for solving environmental problems?

An owner of an egg farm killed 17,000 fish through pollution of a local stream. What are some ways you think the owner could be punished?

In Ohio, the punishment for such action is based on the type and number of fish killed and on how much time officers spend investigating the cause. The owner of the egg farm was fined $6,259 for the pollution.

What are your feelings about this punishment?
Does it change your feelings to know that a milk-processing plant killed 78,000 fish and paid a fine of $1,113?

Do you think it is more important for a government to make laws to protect the environment or to develop industry to keep people employed?

Talk about the negative effects of cars on the environment. Make some suggestions for solving this problem.

What are you doing to help the environment?

What can you do to save water and energy in your home?

_____

*Did you think of these?

- Population growth
- Use of natural resources
- Climate changes
- Air quality
- Waste disposal
- Deforestation

Don't Believe Everything You Hear

How often do you listen to or read the news?

What kinds of news are you interested in?

Where do you get your news?

Sixty-five percent of Americans get their news from television; 21%, from newspapers; 9%, from the radio; 2%, from the Internet.

How do most people get news in your country?

What kinds of newspapers are available in your country?

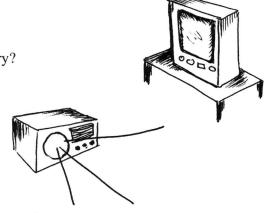

- What languages are they written in?
- How often are they published?
- What is contained in the papers?
- How much do they cost?
- How are they distributed?

What kinds of television news are available in your country?

Do you think news reporters should be able to take people's pictures and use what people say without permission?

What are some news stories that you think should not be shown on television or in newspapers?

Are there some subjects that are not allowed in your country?

What are the differences among an article in a newspaper, an article in a magazine, and an article in a tabloid?

You Be the Judge

What crimes are most common in your country?

What is the punishment for stealing in your country?

Does it make a difference if
- it is $100 or $100,000 that is stolen?
- a weapon is used?
- the thief had a special need for the money?
- the thief had stolen before?
- the thief is a child or an adult?

Do you think parents should be responsible for the crimes of their children? Why? Is prison an effective punishment? Is capital punishment?

What are some things you do to protect yourself from crime?

Stella Liebeck, age 74, purchased coffee at a McDonald's Drive-Thru. Stella placed the coffee cup between her knees to open it to add cream and sugar. The coffee spilled on Stella. She was severely burned and spent eight days in the hospital. When McDonald's refused to pay her medical expenses, Stella sued.

What are your thoughts about this true story?

If you were the judge in this case, what would you have done?

Would this happening be a crime in your country?

Stella was awarded $160,000 for her pain and $480,000 as punishment to McDonald's. Do you think this was a fair settlement? Why?

How do you think the amount of money awarded in such a case should be determined?

One Person's Trash Is Another Person's Treasure

Describe the typical contents of a trash can/waste basket/garbage can in your country.

- What do people throw away?
- How is it different from what people throw away in the United States?

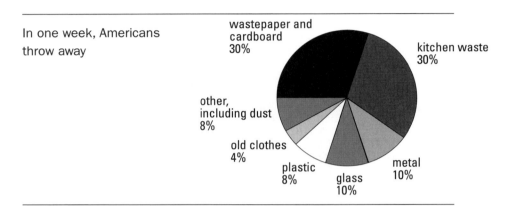

In one week, Americans throw away

wastepaper and cardboard 30%

kitchen waste 30%

other, including dust 8%

old clothes 4%

plastic 8%

glass 10%

metal 10%

Do you consider yourself wasteful?

The average American throws away 1,300 pounds of garbage a year. In addition, Americans throw away over seven million cars each year.

What kinds of food do you waste most often?

Do you think children should be made to eat all the food on their plates? Why?

What did your parents say to encourage you to "clean your plate"?

The average U.S. home wastes 10–15% of the food it buys. The most wasted foods are vegetables, bakery goods, fruit, fast food, and red meat.

What can you do to reduce the amount of waste that you produce?

What items are recycled in your country?

What items do you recycle?

Sixty-seven percent of Americans say they recycle one or more types of items—cans, paper, glass, or plastic. Thirty-three percent say they do not recycle.

Part J
CULTURAL ISSUES

All Good Things Must Come to an End

How and when is New Year's celebrated in your country?

- Describe any special New Year's colors.
- Describe any special New Year's foods.
- Describe any special New Year's greetings.
- Describe any special New Year's traditions.

At midnight on New Year's Eve in the United States, people kiss or honk car horns.

Americans often make New Year's resolutions, promises to themselves to improve some area of their life. For example, some people resolve to eat more vegetables, to exercise more, or to look for a new job.

Seventy-nine percent of Americans' New Year's resolutions concern spending less money. Seventy-one percent resolve to lose weight or get in better shape.

What New Year's resolutions would you make?

What suggestions do you have to help people keep their resolutions?

Describe another special holiday in your country.

Silence Is Golden

Talk about ways people communicate without words.*

How does nonverbal communication differ between the United States and your country?

Discuss the use of all types of nonverbal communication in your country.

How do people greet each other?

How far apart do people stand?

How much eye contact do they make?

How much do they touch one another?

How do they communicate

- "I don't know"?
- "Hello"?
- "Be quiet"?
- "OK"?
- "He's crazy"?
- "I don't understand"?
- "I forgot"?

In general, what percent of a message given in person do you think is nonverbal?

Researchers say that 93% of a message given in person is nonverbal—that only 7% of a message comes from the words used, 38% from the sound of the voice, and 55% from visual messages.

---

* Did you think of these?

- Eye contact
- Gestures
- Facial expressions
- Posture
- Body positions
- Movement
- Distance
- Music

Finders Keepers, Losers Weepers

Have you ever lost anything? For example, have you ever left anything on a bus or subway or train? Talk about some things you have lost or misplaced.

What items do you think people most commonly lose or misplace?

With a partner, list the ten items you think are most frequently left on subways and buses in New York City, the ten items you believe are most commonly lost in your country, and the ten items you think are most frequently left on buses and subways (the Tube) in London.

New York City	Home Country	London

When you have completed your list, turn to the next page.

The New York City Transit Authority keeps a list of all the items left on New York City subways and buses. The ten most common types of lost property on the New York City subways and buses are

1. backpacks
2. radios/Walkmans
3. eyeglasses
4. wallets and purses
5. cameras
6. keys
7. cellular phones
8. watches
9. in-line skates
10. jewelry

Moving up quickly are electronic calculators and laptop computers.

According to the London Transport Lost Property Office, the items most regularly left behind by passengers on London's buses and subways in 1998 were

1. books, checkbooks, credit cards
2. handbags and purses
3. items of clothing
4. cases and bags
5. umbrellas
6. jewelry, cameras, and radios
7. keys
8. glasses
9. gloves
10. miscellaneous

Were your lists for New York and London similar to the official lists?

Discuss possible reasons why the New York and London lists differ.

Was the list from your country similar to either of the official lists? What might account for the differences?

What does the list from the New York City Transit Authority tell you about the culture of the United States?

Talk about the possession you would most hate to lose.

Do You Swear to Tell the Truth?

Have you ever told a lie?

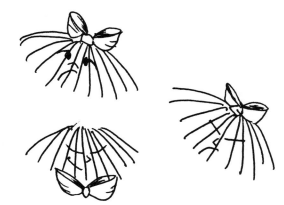

- When?
- Under what circumstances?
- Was it planned?

Did you ever lie as a child?

- Were you ever found out?
- What were the consequences?
- How did you feel?

Are there any times when you would lie?

If a doctor told you someone you love is dying, and if that person asked you to tell him or her the truth, would you?

If you were the doctor of a patient with cancer whose situation seemed hopeless, would you tell the patient so?

Would it matter if

- the patient was young or old?
- the patient was male or female?
- the patient had a strong or weak character?
- the patient had other problems, such as job, family, marital, or financial?

Ninety-six percent of the patients at a New York City hospital agreed that even when medical news is bad, a patient should be told about it.

What would you say if

- friends who invited you to their home for dinner asked your opinion of the food and you thought it was awful or you couldn't eat it because of your religion?
- your friend asked you about his/her hair cut and you thought it looked terrible?
- your friend gave you a birthday present that you did not like?

What are some situations in your country in which people might not always tell the truth?

Do you trust your friends to always tell you the truth?

Do you always tell the truth to your friends?

Part K
CHOICES

Once Upon a Time

Take turns telling as many stories as you can in the time allotted. Choose a different opener for each story.

When I opened the door, I saw a basket . . .

The man said I had won $1,000,000, but . . .

I could see the object moving near my bedroom door . . .

This morning my alarm clock didn't go off . . .

One Sunday I decided to do something really unusual . . .

"You'll need a hammer," said the man behind the counter . . .

As a rule, you should never speak to strangers, but . . .

While I was watching TV . . .

Just as the professor entered the classroom . . .

I could smell something burning . . .

The driver was really angry because . . .

I called to ask my friend to go out, but . . .

You Can't Have Your Cake and Eat It Too

For your birthday, would you rather have as a gift a dog, a bicycle, a new coat, or something else? Why?

    When are gifts exchanged in your country? What types of gifts are exchanged?

If you had an evening free, would you spend it watching TV, being with family, reading, talking to friends, going to a movie, or dining out? Why?

    Would your choice be different in your country?

    Which do you think is the top choice of Americans?*

Would you rather win the Nobel Prize, make a lot of money, have a wonderful home life, or enjoy lifelong health? Why?

If you were going on vacation, would you rather go to the beach, the mountains, or the city? Why?

    Would you prefer to spend most of your vacation time resting and relaxing or involved in activities and sightseeing?

According to a Gallup poll, 67% of Americans prefer to spend their time sightseeing and being active, while 32% prefer just to rest and relax.

Discuss some of the activities people can do or sights they can see while on vacation in your country.

What is one household chore you prefer not to do? Why?

If you were going to stay home and watch television today would you watch sports, cooking, a movie, news and weather, or something else?

    Describe your favorite television program.

*Americans' top choice for evening recreation is watching television at 31%. They rank other recreational activities as follows:

being with family	20%	going to a movie	11%
reading	18%	visiting friends	6%
dining out	15%		

Would you rather

be able to end all wars or all diseases?

be famous for one day or rich for one day?

live in a world without wheels or a world without electricity?

save from a burning building a priceless Michelangelo piece of art or your child's pet kitten?

work for your brother or sister or for your best friend?

be stuck in an elevator for two days with someone who won't talk at all or with someone who talks too much?

A Penny for Your Thoughts

Take turns selecting and talking about topics from the following lists.

Activities, such as parties
Bananas or other foods
Children or pets
Driving or modern conveniences
Education or learning English
Football or other sports
Grandparents or other relatives
Homes or homelands
Internet activities or computer uses
Jets or other modes of transportation
Knee bends or other exercises
Love or another emotion
Manners or behavior differences
Narcotics or medicines
Outstanding people or events
Pumpkin carving or other customs
Quarters or other money
Radios or news sources
Sunshine or other weather
Telephoning or other ways to communicate
Unemployment or employment
Vacuuming or other household chores
Weddings or other ceremonies
X rays or hospitals
Yard sales or shopping
Zoos or trips

You might want to talk about

- the positive and negative aspects of your topic
- your personal experiences with your topic
- the usefulness or value of your topic
- when you would experience this topic
- how this topic is different in different cultures

And They All Lived Happily Ever After

**Take turns telling as many stories as you can in the time allotted.
Choose a different concluding sentence for each story.**

I will never answer the telephone again.

So I jumped up and answered the door.

And that is how I got my new shirt.

And I turned the alarm off and went back to sleep.

I know I'll never do that again!

Fortunately, it was all a dream.

Next week, I'm going to try again.

What a vacation!

My friends are still laughing.

And I made it all by myself.

I can't believe they only wanted six dollars for it!

I never thought I would win.

Part L

TRAVEL ISSUES

Everything but the Kitchen Sink

Everyone has a method for packing a suitcase. How do you pack? If you were packing one suitcase for a trip of several days, how would you pack?

Would you make a list first?

Would you lay everything out first?

What would you put in the suitcase first and where would you put it?

How would you pack shirts?

How would you pack shoes?

What would you put on top in the suitcase?

Do you have any special packing tips?

According to experts, you should

- pack heavy items, such as shoes, in the bottom of your suitcase
- stuff small items in shoes
- place shoes in plastic bags
- roll undergarments and use them to fill spaces
- pack shirts buttoned
- fold or roll clothes
- seal items that might leak (in plastic bags)
- place lightest clothing on top in a suitcase

Do you tend to overpack? Underpack? Why?

How do you identify your suitcase?

When you came to the United States, who packed for you?

Describe a special possession you brought with you in your suitcase.

It's a Small, Small World

Describe your last vacation.

Describe your dream vacation.

Where would you go?

When would you go?

How would you get there?

Who would you go with?

What would you do?

Two out of three Americans say that their ideal vacation would be to keep moving, while 31% would prefer to spend it in just one place. Seventy-three percent would choose to vacation in a new place rather than return to a place they have been before.

Eleven percent of Americans prefer to stay at home while on vacation; 17% prefer the beach; 10% prefer the mountains.

Most Americans vacation during the month of August.

Sixty-seven percent of American vacationers drive to their vacation spot; 25% fly.

Sixty-four percent of Americans vacation with their families.

Talk about some interesting things you have done on vacation.

What souvenirs have you bought?

It's a Lemon

How do people get to work in your country?

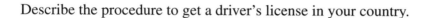

According to a Gallup poll of Americans, 87% drive their own car or truck to work, 4% walk or bike, 2% take the bus, 1% use the subway, and 1% carpool.

Describe your country's roads and highways.

- What types of cars do people drive?
- Which side of the road do people drive on?
- What other vehicles are on the roads besides cars?

Describe the procedure to get a driver's license in your country.

Tell about a car or motorcycle you, a friend, or a family member own or would like to own.

What makes you choose a particular vehicle?

- Friends' recommendations?
- Advertising?
- Ratings?
- Persuasive salesmen?
- Color?

How do people buy new and used cars in your country?

Sixty-five percent of Americans buying a car buy a used car. Thirty-four percent purchase their used car from a private owner; 49% buy one from dealerships.

How do people in your country care for their cars?

Twenty-two percent of Americans wash their cars weekly; nearly half of them wash them by hand at home.

Thirty-two percent of Americans change their own oil.

Discuss what you would do if you had a flat tire.

Mirror, Mirror on the Wall,
Who's the Fairest of Them All?

What have you noticed about car license plates in the United States?

Many people use their car license plates to convey a message about themselves. These are called vanity plates. Can you decipher the messages of the vanity plates?*

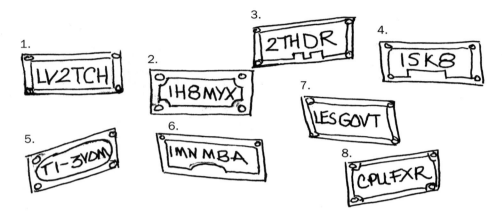

What would you want on your license plate?

Why do people purchase vanity plates?

What other ways do people display vanity or pride in themselves?**

In what ways do people attempt to improve their appearance?

---

*Here are some hints.

1. an instructor	5. mirror image
2. used to be married	6. new Harvard grad
3. not an MD	7. political statement
4. winter sport	8. computer repair

**Did you think of these?

· Appearance
· Choice of cars and careers
· Size and location of home
· Choice of schools and universities

Every year in the United States, nearly 1 million women and 100,000 men have plastic surgery to improve their appearance. The most common surgeries are liposuction (fat removal), breast augmentation (increase), eyelid surgery, and facelifts.

What occupations have high prestige in your country? In the United States?***

What schools and universities have high prestige in your country? In the United States?

***The most prestigious occupations in the United States are

- doctor
- scientist
- teacher
- clergyman
- military officer
- policeman
- Member of Congress
- engineer
- architect
- lawyer

(Information from Harris Poll, Aug. 10–14, 2000.)

Tell It Like It Is

Have you ever noticed the bumper stickers that are on many American cars?

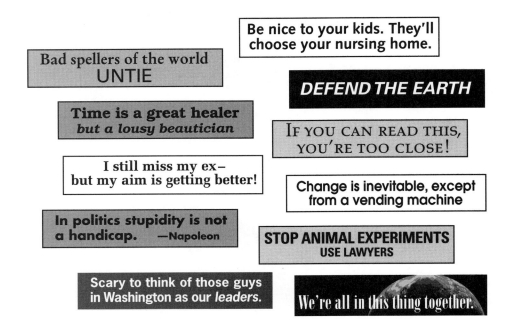

bumper

Be nice to your kids. They'll choose your nursing home.

Bad spellers of the world
UNTIE

DEFEND THE EARTH

Time is a great healer
but a lousy beautician

IF YOU CAN READ THIS,
YOU'RE TOO CLOSE!

I still miss my ex–
but my aim is getting better!

Change is inevitable, except
from a vending machine

In politics stupidity is not
a handicap.   —Napoleon

STOP ANIMAL EXPERIMENTS
USE LAWYERS

Scary to think of those guys
in Washington as our *leaders*.

We're all in this thing together.

Look at the bumper stickers. What types of messages do you see? What do these messages tell you about some Americans?

What else do Americans put on their cars?

Have you noticed the university stickers in some rear windows? Why do you think people put them there?

What do people in your country do to distinguish their cars? What decorations or things do they put on or in their cars?

How are cars in your country decorated differently than cars in the United States? Why do you think this is so?

Part M
LIFE CHANGES

For Better or for Worse

Who chooses the person you marry?

Who has to approve of the marriage?

Who plans the wedding?

Describe a wedding ceremony in your country.

Where does it take place?

Who pays for it?

What are the average costs?

What people are usually invited?

What is the usual age of the bride and groom?

Describe the clothing worn by the wedding party.

What time, day, and month do most weddings take place?

What gifts are commonly given?

Is money or property exchanged between the two families?

Is there a celebration after the ceremony?

Does the couple go on a honeymoon?

Discuss any other wedding customs.

In the United States, the average wedding includes 188 guests and costs more than $19,000.

The median age for a first marriage in the United States is 25 for women, 27 for men.

June is the month of 11.3% of American weddings; 10.9% are in August.

Traditional American wedding gifts are china, silver, crystal, small appliances, small electronics, cookware, and linens.

The most popular honeymoon spots for American newlyweds are Hawaii, Florida, and the Caribbean.

Baby Talk

Share your opinions about having children.

- At what age should people have children?
- How many children per family are ideal?
- How many years are best between children in a family?
- How important is the sex of the child?

Describe your country's special traditions surrounding the birth of a child.

- What is done before the birth of a child to help new parents prepare?
- Are there some good dates or years to have children? Why?
- Where is the baby born?
- Who attends the birth?
- How is the birth announced?
- Where does the baby sleep?
- What foods can or cannot be eaten by the pregnant or nursing mother?
- What other beliefs govern the behavior of the mother and child?
- What gifts are given to the baby?

How are baby names chosen in your country?

Can parents choose any name they wish?

What are some common names for babies born now in your country?

Some very common names for babies born now in the United States are:

James	Emily
Matthew	Sarah
Michael	Samantha
Christopher	Hannah
Nicholas	Ashley

Who should be most responsible for the care of a baby? Why?

What do you remember about the care of babies in your home?

Here Today, Gone Tomorrow

Tell about a time when you moved to a new home or apartment.

How often have you moved?

_____

People move frequently in the United States. Forty-three million Americans, or 16.7% of the population, move to a new home or apartment each year.

The average American moves at least 12 times, or an average of once every five to six years.

_____

How often do people move in your country? For what reasons?

_____

The top reasons why people move in the United States are

- to transfer to a new job
- to get a better house

_____

What are the advantages and disadvantages of moving to a new place?

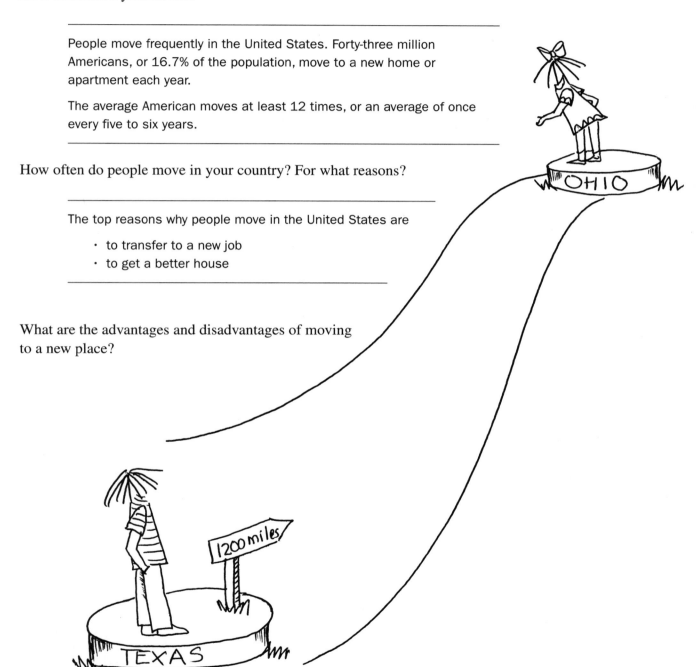

How do people in your country move their possessions?

_____

In the United States, about 20% of people use a moving company;
another 20% use a truck rental company.

_____

When do children leave home in your country?

_____

In the United States, children often leave home at age 18. Only 15% of
American men between the ages of 25 and 34 still live at home.

In Spain and Italy, more than 50% of men ages 25–29 live at home.

_____

In your country, do most grown children live
near their parents or grandparents?

Describe the choices of living arrangements available to grown children in your country.

_____

Grown American children often live far away from their parents and
grandparents.

_____

Gone but Not Forgotten

Describe the special rites or ceremonies that take place when a person dies in your country.

Where do they take place?

What people attend?

Do children attend funerals? At what age?

What clothes do people wear following a death?

What stories are told during funerals?

What happens to the body after death?

How are people notified of the death?

Do people send cards, money, or flowers or bring food for the family?

What other customs in your country help comfort people who have lost a loved one?

Discuss your beliefs about life after death.

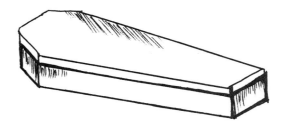